My Ex(s)
Are Not Going To
Like This One

In loving memory of my Exes, who may not be dead but probs wish they were now.

Maria Daniela Rodriguez

AuthorHouse™ UK
1663 Liberty Drive
Bloomington, IN 47403 USA
www.authorhouse.co.uk
UK TFN: 0800 0148641 (Toll Free inside the UK)
UK Local: 02036 956322 (+44 20 3695 6322 from outside the UK)

Because of the dynamic nature of the Internet, any web addresses or links contained in this book may have changed
since publication and may no longer be valid. The views expressed in this work are solely those of the author and do
not necessarily reflect the views of the publisher, and the publisher hereby disclaims any responsibility for them.

Any people depicted in stock imagery provided by Getty Images are models,
and such images are being used for illustrative purposes only.
Certain stock imagery © Getty Images.

This book is printed on acid-free paper.

ISBN: 979-8-8230-8614-1 (sc)
ISBN: 979-8-8230-8615-8 (e)

Library of Congress Control Number: 2024901219

Print information available on the last page.

Published by AuthorHouse 03/15/2024

authorHOUSE®

Preface

Hey, hey!

I hope this book finds you well.

I just wanted to say before you dive right into the trenches of my soul that by the end of it, you'll either feel my pain or think I am utterly insane.

But one thing to note about me is that I love constructive criticism, so don't let the fear of potentially hurting my feelings stop you from reading this!

It's okay.

I'd say about 65.7 per cent of these were written on public transport, work breaks, lesson rooms, places I should've been definitely paying *more* attention to.

I don't want to sell you the idea that I was dramatically crying on the floor of my bedroom. That simply wasn't the case—although I have done that too, just not whilst writing.

A lot of these poem-like texts are the product of reflections I've had about people, experiences, and things within myself, essentially.

I hope you're following.
I guess what I'm trying to say is that this book was written on impulse. All the thoughts I share are genuine to how I felt at the time, regardless of how I may feel about them nowadays.

I'll always love reminiscing over past emotions/experiences and discovering ways in which they did or didn't shape me as a person. I think there's something, sure quite masochistic, but cool about that, no? Like learning from the bad, even if you feel like you're the bad one a lot of the time.

And you know what? Even if you read this and we don't click and you think that you've wasted your money on this peculiar twenty-one-year-old's book, just remember, *at least I'm honest*.

And I don't like a lot of my thoughts either.

See? We'd still be able to relate to each other on something.
Even if it's on my self-deprecation.

Enjoy. xoxoxo

Meraki

(v.) to do something with soul, creativity, or love; to leave a piece and essence of yourself in work.

You Should've Known I'm Crazy

Can't wait for y'all to read this,
Reiterate that I'm insane.
But babes, are you not impressed
I chose to profit off this pain?

Don't worry; it's not all bad!

Some of them might be brutal,
But I swear on my life they're 100 per cent truthful.

I even wrote a few apologies
With reason and a glass of wine.
I think it's official:
I've gone mad over time.

Forelsket

(n.) the euphoria you experience when you are first falling in love.

I have always been one to fall in love with a fantasy, the potential in a stranger. One glance and a seed of hope is planted.

Ninety per cent of the time, this seed never blossoms;
it's *hollow* on the inside.

Nevertheless, it doesn't stop me from watering it daily and placing it in the sun.

I watch over it every day, waiting for a sign of life to peak through the stubborn soil.

Days, weeks, sometimes even months go by, and the soil starts to harden and dry.

This is usually when I get desperate and excessively water it with tears until it turns into mud.

But the mud makes my hands and clothes dirty, and I start to wonder why I feel so dehydrated.
So I change approach.

I dim my thoughts and shine my brightest light, hoping this might make it right.

But my light is too strong, and I end up burning the field where all my forgotten seeds lay.

I'm the Queen of Hopeless Seeds.

I Like to Read Books about Love

I like to read books about love,
binge-watch films about it too.
I like to immerse myself in series
that glamorise hopping into the dating pool.

They make it sound fun and exciting,
sometimes even thrilling and a bit spicy.

And I find myself fantasising if one day
it'll happen to me too.
If one day I'll experience the greatness of love
with all the twists and turns that come with being a fool.

But then I'm reminded that the world I live in doesn't match this fictional reality,
that living in my own head is probably not good for my sanity.

Nevertheless, I like to believe that I will find someone that will match my loving wits,
someone who will understand the weight of the words that come from a writer's fingertips.

I Want Someone to Grow Old With

I want to be loved by someone who gets excited about the little things,
Someone I can travel and explore the world with.
I want to be loved by someone who will do karaoke with me,
Someone who is not afraid to be childishly silly.
I want to be loved by someone who is not afraid to take risks,
Someone who holds my heart and caresses it with their fingertips.
I want to be loved by someone who makes me feel whole,
Someone who knows how to touch my body as well as my soul.
I want to be loved by someone I can endlessly write about,
Someone who will search for me in every small or big crowd.
I want to be loved by someone who will not make me question my worth,
Someone who will still think I am beautiful when I am wrinkly and old.

Redamancy

(n.) the act of loving the one who loves you; a love returned in full.

Cheese String

I love nicknaming my crushes;
it's a very typical thing for me to do.
And funny enough, cheese string was the one I chose for you.

It really wasn't that hard.
in fact, I didn't even have to think at all—
curly blond hair, skinny, tall.

I kinda knew I was in trouble from the moment we first spoke,
and to be honest, I'm not really sure how it started.
I don't think I even noticed when the ice broke.

But maybe that's because it wasn't needed.

I mean, our conversations did have an easy flow, and with similar interests, my curiosity
began to grow.

Your jokes were actually really funny.
But that's something I'll never let you know, because although we have similar humour,
I am still the roasting pro.

And speaking of roasts,
I think it's fair that you're due one.
See, I've been way too nice,
and you're still shaped like a ruler.

I can actually picture you reading this,
half smile and all,
just please don't ruin my rhymes
with your mumbling northern tone.

Also, thanks for the spoon;
it was actually extremely useful.
At least up until I lost it.
But do I get points for being truthful?

And before you get cocky!

I'm not making moves (behave)
or looking for validation.
I'm just an overachiever
who made some little observations.

Wonderwall

(adj.) someone you find yourself thinking about all the time; a person you are completely infatuated with.

The Soundtrack to Your Life

Not every failed connection is a waste of time.

Some people are only meant to be doted notes in the song of your life.

They'll serve their purpose and extend your tune for a while.

Help you rewrite old symphonies that'll lead to new rhythms and rhymes.

You'll confidently skip through these new tabs together,

Until one day, you'll reach the end, and their musical touch will sever.

But even then, you'll still carry on grooving, maybe a bit dazed and confused.

But I promise you'll find a new rhythm,

Another temporary blues.

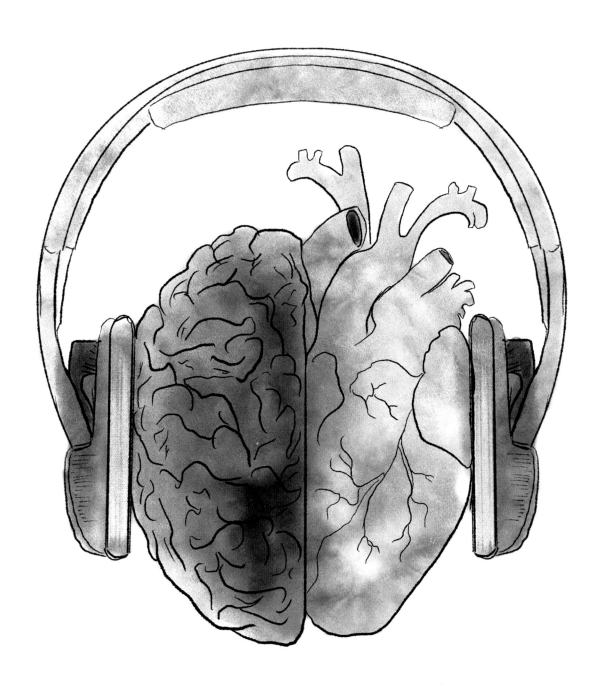

Kilig

(n.) the rush or the inexplicable joy one feels after seeing or experiencing something romantic.

You Can't Put Love in a Box

Love is something so simple yet so complex.

We talk about it all the time, about our wishes, dreams, hopes, and expectations.

We create our own versions of what it's like to love and feel loved, disregarding that you can't box up such an unpredictable and carnal feeling.

We get frustrated when someone's way of loving doesn't fit our own premade box.

Whether it's too much and it overflows, leaving us feeling heavy and weak; or whether it's too small, and the gaps of air make you feel like you're floating around their mis-matched passion as you desperately try to fill it with your own.

You can't put love in a pre-existent box.

Truth be told, the feeling of being in love is subjective.

Some wear their hearts on their sleeves and won't be afraid to show you how madly indulged in your aura they are.

Whereas others are more reserved and will rather show it in small gestures, whether it's acts of service, patience, or simply showing gratitude for your company.

The beauty of being in love with another being comes from being able to mould and shape it as a unit. To start from scratch and learn how to create your own unique container which won't be the same as others you might've built before.

This makes every love you experience its own, with different corners and edges, lines and curves, weights and heights.

You shouldn't put love in a box; you should use it as a tool to create one in which you can hold the memories you made and lessons you learnt as a partnership.

Dystychinphobia

(n.) the fear of hurting someone.

Cheese String Pt 2

You're a peculiar person with your own quirks and ways of being.
You don't come across as a fake, or in other words, deceiving.

You're funny and sweet,
maybe a bit childishly nerdy,
but I hope you're still making dry puns by the time you hit 30.

Kindness is timeless, and it shows in your face.
So listen to me when I say
you really don't need to change.

You're more charming than you think.
I hope you find a girl who makes you feel extraordinary and unique.

I hope she sees what I see
and reminds you every day
that you're loved and cared for
and that she'll never go away.

I hope she's the pollen you need
to make sweet honey
out of every dead weed.

I hope she makes you feel more confident in yourself,
that she shows you you're special
and not just like everyone else.

I'll support you from afar,
secretly wishing it could be me.
But I know that's not possible,
so I'll stay hidden in the trees.

I'm glad we're friends,
even if we speak in riddles or every few weeks.
I enjoy our innocent banter and your sarcastic critiques.

Tacenda

(n.) things better left unsaid; matters to be passed over in silence.

The flowers you sent for me were laced with poisonous weeds,
a misleadingly sweet gesture,
An attempt to make me bleed.

Agliophobia

(n.) The fear of being hurt.

Red Roses

I have always loved flowers, specifically white roses. Something about the simplicity of the colour blended in with the most beautiful of shapes brought peace to my damaged soul. But it was at 15 when I realised that even the most beautiful of roses grow to become rotten. When his thorn-covered hands touched mine, I bled until his white petals were covered with my cries for help.

My blood was invisible to others but vibrant to him; the tighter I held on, the deeper into my soul he went.

My perfect white rose was now fully red, and my hands were left with the scars of his harsh words and unstable temper.

I wondered how long I would have to keep watering his roots to bring back the white rose I once planted. But it was then I noticed that he was never white; his petals were poisoned from the inside, and his paleness reflected his own cruelty. He was unable to be his true colour and therefore drained mine until he created the perfect facade, a classic red rose.

I hate red roses.

How sad is it that you worshipped my body
but demonised my soul.
That I thought of you as a saint
when you treated me like a whore.

My soul deserves to be touched too.

If Those Walls Could Talk

If those walls could talk,
I'm sure we'd scream the same pain,
we'd point at our twinning cracks,
and joke about the damage he did create.

If those walls could talk,
they'd recount every breath they heard me take
or every time I'd turn to it for comfort,
only to find myself burying my face.

If those walls could talk,
they'd tell you about how when I got scared, I would scrape at its blue paint.
How I'd use it to keep my hands busy
until he finished shouting the words he couldn't just easily say.

If those walls could talk,
they'd say how hard I'd try to get him to calm down,
how I learnt how to cry silently
and not be too loud.

If only those walls could talk,
they'd be the ones to avenge me.
They'd be the ones testifying in court.
They'd be the *only* ones able to defend me.
He's punching the walls again.

Sometimes I ponder if even a fraction of you misses me, even if it's just a tad.
But I forget who this is addressed to,
forget you're too mature to ever feel sad.

You don't recall my jokes,
not that they ever made you laugh.
You don't reminisce over my voice;
you never noticed its subtle rasp.

But,

I bet you remember me naked.
I bet you remember me gasp,
lying in a quarter-sized bed
with my legs split in half.

Now you're reenacting the scene
with a clenched jaw and fixed gaze.
Are you really that surprised your hand
can't keep up with my pace?

You only ever think of me when you masturbate.

Slut

(n.) a woman with the morals of a man.

You Went on a Date Today

I'm really angry today,
frustrated and confused.
You are no longer a problem for me to worry about, but the *disrespect* that followed our breakup still makes me feel blue.
You went on a date today,
5 weeks after we broke up.
Funny, isn't it,
2.5 years turned into dust?

I saw it coming from miles away.
I even told you how this is what you would do.
I remember you were offended.
Laughed in my face, like it was all just a joke to you.

You told me you loved me deeply
and that I would regret crossing you out of my heart.
But do you really think I want to be with someone who finds me oh so easy to discard?

I mean, that is the main reason I left:
I never felt special.
I knew you wouldn't hesitate to move on to the next.

In fact, you even told me that too!
How you were going to the gym again
just in case I'd leave you. (LOL.)
Pathetic really, if you ask me, how you think flexing your muscles will make it easy to replace my legacy.

Think I'm finally seeing things in a clearer light; this is who you are,
and you know what?

That's fine!

I hope you fuck all the girls you want
and gain all the bragging rights.
Post it on your private story if that's what is going to help you sleep at night.
You're embarrassing yourself in front of everyone's eyes,
so let me sit back and enjoy the show,
And
oh, don't forget to smile ;)

Morosis

(n.) the stupidest of stupidities.

I know my name bothers you now

I know my name cuts to the bone and rips you open somehow

I know my name haunts you in your sleep

I know that you can't help that it makes a comeback in your dreams

I know my name is talked about in your house

I know that deep down I'm all you think about

I know my name drips like poison as you spit it out of your mouth

We both know my name holds a legacy that will always follow you around.

You never thought I'd have that much impact until I left.

Hypophrenia

(Greek)

(n.) A vague feeling of sadness, seemingly without any cause.

"I didn't ask you to."
You're right, you did not.
Forgive me for giving my all
To someone who made my efforts feel small.

How can you be so ungrateful?

I'm Tired of Waiting

I'm tired of waiting, waiting for you to call, waiting for you to make time for me, waiting for you to remember me at all.

I always made excuses for your lack of sensibility; I guess it was easier to lie to myself than to admit I was not a priority.

I'm tired of arguing about feeling left out.

I'm tired of crying and dealing with doubts.

Kinda silly how I stayed up late,

Even when you didn't ask me to;

You didn't like doing that for me.

You always said you had things to work through.

You said you felt suffocated,

that you're never sure when to fit me into your schedule, but that's not what bothered me.

It was your lack of communication that was detrimental.

You never make time for me
The way I do for you.
You say you're busy,
That you have other things to do.
But I didn't know gaming and sleeping
Counted as extraneous work.
But it's fine, I'll ignore it.
I'm sure you don't mean to neglect to put me first.
After all, your thumbs must be exhausted
To not be able to text me back.
But it's fine because you won your game,
So I'll cut you some slack.
And honestly, you should invest in a new mattress
So you can get some proper sleep.
I know 12 hours of snoring is not enough
For you to have the energy to speak to me.

Keep on ignoring me.

Yonderly

(adj.) mentally or emotionally distant; absent-minded.

Now my chest feels heavy, and my heart frowns in disappointment every time our friends tell me about your life.

You're becoming a stranger over time.

I'll remember our travels fondly,
Eating pizza in Italy
And gyros in Greece.
I'll remember your hometown,
Your childhood pictures
On your grandma's fridge.
I'll remember Zakopane,
Being excited about the cheese
And the pierogis your mum made.
I wish I would've asked for the recipe.
I kept all the pictures
For the photo album we never made.
I can't bring myself to get rid of them.
Not all memories are worth being erased

Hiraeth

(n.) the feeling of being homesick for a home one is not able to return to; homesickness pertaining to a home that never was.

I know my name bothers you now

I know my name cuts to the bone and rips you open somehow

I know my name haunts you in your sleep

I know that you can't help that it makes a comeback in your dreams

I know my name is talked about in your house

I know that deep down I'm all you think about

I know my name drips like poison as you spit it out of your mouth

We both know my name holds a legacy that will always follow you around.

You never thought I'd have that much impact until I left.

"I Want to Date a White Blonde Girl"

Your friend told me the type of girl you're looking for now.
"I want to date a white blonde girl."
So original and predictable somehow.
So you want to date your mum?
You know, Freud would be proud.
Genuinely not shocked those words rolled out of your mouth.
Guess my tan skin and chocolate eyes
Are not necessarily your type.
I hope you enjoy your lemon herb chicken with a side of plain rice.
Sorry, that was nasty.
Maybe a bit controversial, unhinged.
I'm sure you'll make beautiful babies,
Keep the bloodline as pure as it is.
I'm sure she'll be beautiful.
Honestly, this is just jealousy talking.
I too wish I had the privilege of always being chosen.

Lesson learnt.
I vow to never fail to put myself first.
I'd rather float through life in peace
Than let another comedian make a joke out of me.
        Joker.

Habromania

(n.) delusions of happiness.

I hate how now I've turned to drinking

How I reach for the bottle to stop myself from thinking

How wine was supposed to be a temporary solution for my anguish

But I carried on sipping until my self-control was tarnished

It doesn't actually make me feel better

It makes me feel worse

I feel so stupid cussing you with slurred words—

      Wine drunk.

I'd have better luck confiding in a wall than in you
At least the walls won't interrupt me
Or give me unwarranted reviews.

 I don't want you to lecture me; I want you to listen.

I murdered my own heart hunting for potential in someone who didn't even care to acknowledge mine.

Anagapesis

(n.) no longer feeling any affection for someone you once loved.

Watch Me Grow

I used to think I wouldn't heal,
that my wounds would stay open
and bleed so brightly
they'd be impossible to conceal.

But months have gone by,
and I barely remember the sound of your voice.
Turns out it wasn't that hard
to fill your void.

I filled it with a new love,
a love that was always there
but that my silly little brain took ages to comprehend.

I fell in love with myself
and all the little things you'd criticised I do.
Turns out my flaws are perfect.
I'm so glad I was able to see it through.

Through your harsh words and unwarranted comments,
I think my potential is what scared you if I'm being honest.

You underestimated the power I had,
and now I want you to watch me burn down every careless word you said to me
that made me sad.

I'm crying again, and I can sense you huff and puff as you shamelessly roll your eyes.
"You're too much for me; I can't deal with this all the time."
Yeah, well babe, shockingly neither can I.
How is it my fault that your words hit like knives?

It's not my fault you never think before you speak.

I Feel Guilty of Giving You My Love

I'm guilty of forgiving you
One too many times.
I'm guilty of staying
Even when you made me cry.
I'm guilty of making excuses
For the behaviour you'd uphold.
I'm guilty of not listening
When my friends told me you were cold.
I'm guilty of defending you
In conversations with my mum on the phone.
I'm guilty of loving you
Even when your heart was made of stone.
I'm guilty of seeing the best
In someone who made me unhappy.
I'm guilty of having been in love with a
Fucking narcissist.

The Current Is Changing

There's a reason why I carry myself the way I do around you.

At the end of the day, your criticism is so heavy on my shoulders, I find myself growing a hunchback of insecurities as I drag my feet towards you.

Most times, I foolishly hope you'll lift some of it off with your reassuring arms, but by the time I reach you, we're lost at sea again, and my eyes have flooded the small boat we're both sailing in.

This is usually when I stand frozen and watch you tie an anchor around my heels as you coldly remark how my pain is a burden to you.

I watch you jump out the nearest window and leave me to drown in my own swirling whooshing waves of sorrow.

You excuse your own behaviour.

You say it's normal, that it's fine.

That the storm is too tumultuous and, therefore, the captain needs to make sacrifices and abandon his crew.

You senselessly remind me of how fully aware you are that swimming in my own sadness is something you taught me how to do quite well.

See, but then it reached the fourteenth time you've helped me perfect this skill.

I recall how I felt my hands swiftly release my heels before I floated back to the surface and routinely checked the temperature of the current I was in.

Could you tell this time was different?

That this time the water was colder, and I came back quicker?

This time I shallowly observed you sunbathing on the shore and wondered what it would be like to let my tears tsunami and destroy your world too; I wonder if then you'd make the same effort to swim back as many times as I do.

Dystychiphobia

(n.) the fear of hurting someone.

I'm healing now,
and I can actually feel it happening.
I no longer growl at your name
or catch myself frowning.

In fact, I barely react.
It's so relieving to know you no longer have the power you had.

I feel so indifferent.

I'm Learning How to Love Myself

I'm learning to appreciate myself,
Cherish every random thought that develops in my mind.
Take pride in my personality
And not just my outsides.
I'm so much more beautiful than what meets the naked eye.
No mirror will ever be able to reflect my morals, honour, or pride.

Kalon

(n.) beauty that is more than skin deep.

"Apologies Mean Nothing"

Now this is something I've always debated within myself.

When I'm angry and someone disappoints me, my rage-filled emotions seem to agree with this statement as I break down every reason as to why the words they speak to me are a lie.

But hypocritically, when I catch myself in the position where "I'm sorry" splashes out of my mouth, I find myself clawing at their forgiveness as I desperately attempt to show them how my regret and disappointment within myself are genuine.

This is because I know that when I say it, I mean it, and I will make sure I show it with my following actions instead of filling the awkward tension with false hopes.

Not everyone does this, which makes the apology they give lose its authenticity and over time, its importance and categorically its meaning.

I think it's hard to accept that someone is wholeheartedly sorry for the actions that led to your heart feeling betrayed and misused. Especially when their actions contradict it.

It takes a lot to be able to forgive someone for the emotional damage they might've caused, and depending on its scale, it's something that can take minutes, days, weeks, months, and sometimes even years.

The way I see it is that even if you don't see authenticity in their apology, you can always apologise to yourself for allowing them to hurt you the way they did. Being able to forgive yourself means everything, even if their untruthful apologies don't.

Reflections

When I look at myself in the mirror,
I never know what exactly it is that I see.
Sometimes I see myself as it is
Or fragments of versions of past mes.

Sometimes when I get a haircut,
I'm reminded of 10-year-old me.
I'm reminded of how my grandma
Would lecture me about how short hair
Is much easier to manage in the heat.

Sometimes when I have my hair up,
I'm reminded of 14-year-old me.
I'm reminded of how she used to hate her face,
How she used to think she had the chubbiest cheeks.

Sometimes when my hair is dyed,
I'm reminded of 16-year-old me.
I'm reminded of how much she needed help,
Of how good she was at pretending.

Sometimes when my hair is wet,
I'm reminded of 18-year-old me.
I'm reminded of the unstable wreck she was,
How I hope she's proud of me.

Sometimes I don't know what it is that I see.
It's never about how people perceive me
But more about whether I like the current version of me.

I Wrote You a Letter

I don't love you anymore. Crazy, right? I didn't see it coming either; actually kinda took me by surprise. Although I know deep down it shouldn't be so much of a shock as you were right. We were too different, and it's not like you were ever much of a rock.

I don't really know how I feel about you anymore; maybe *indifferent* is the right word, which is so weird considering how in love with you I was before. I used to think you had the most unique name, but now it just sounds so ordinary, so mundane.

Sometimes I get sad at how my feelings drastically changed, but then I remember the reasons as to why I chose to walk away.

I don't regret the effort I put in or all the love I let you take. I just feel disappointed it took me so long to realise we didn't share a common mentality.

See, I used your favourite word there; mentality is something you always used to talk about. You were the one to see things "logically", and I was always the one to pour my heart out.

I used to like this dynamic; I used to think it made perfect sense. But confiding in you was hard, and I always felt incredibly tense. I still remember how I took the blame when you told me my tears were overwhelming; I remember I apologised for my sadness. I mean, your speeches were always very compelling.

I know you always saw me as extremely emotional, and I guess I'm proving you kinda right. But realistically, how was I supposed to feel when you barely looked me in the eye? I'm not saying you were horrible; you are a decent person, and I know can be kind..

But that's no excuse for the careless words you'd say to me when I was "wasting your time". You never wanted to talk when things were off; in fact, you'd just leave it for days and make it 10x worse.

So don't act like my leaving took you by surprise. I always expressed my feelings; it's not my fault you didn't care to read the signs. You told me you'd change, that you saw a future by my side, but your actions fell short and the trust we built was no longer in sight.

The changes never happened, things just stayed the same, it was either the bare minimum or barely talking for days.

I should've seen it coming how you wouldn't even notice my heart was failing but part of me really wishes you did something when the seasons were changing.

But that's done and dusted now, nothing else you can do. I'll never be yours again but just know that I forgive you.

Finifugal

(adj.) hating endings; of someone who tries to avoid or prolong the final moments of a story, relationship and some other journey

Acknowledgments:

I have sat around twiddling my thumbs, trying to put into to words how ever so grateful I am for the genuine support I've felt during these past 5 years of my life. Half a decade ago I could only dream about what it would be like to write my own book.
I am 4 lifetimes away from the girl I was at the time and I say that with the most compassion and love for my younger self.

I will always cherish the girl that thought the world couldn't hurt her. She is loved by me. But she is also loved and supported by those around her.

To my mum who always let me cry without judgment and heard me when no one else did, You are the reason I am the woman I am today, and I will always aspire to be as kind and as strong as you. *You painted me a world full of colour when our reality was black and white* ;). I am eternally grateful for you.

To my stepdad, who *allegedly* always reminded me how he would break the legs of anyone who tried to hurt me. Thank you for always pushing me forward.

To my best buddies who were there for me when I didn't want to be alone, you are so fucking annoying. But I love you, so so so much. I appreciate every single one of you more than you'll ever know.

Who knows, maybe one day I'll write a book about you? A sweeter one this time? But only if you behave, please.

Thank you for everything, I genuinely am beyond thankful for all of you xx

Printed in the United States
by Baker & Taylor Publisher Services